Alligators

by **Steven Otfinoski**

Marshall Cavendish
Benchmark
New York

Thanks to Kent A. Vilet, Ph.D., coordinator of biological sciences
at the University of Florida,
for his expert reading of this manuscript.

Marshall Cavendish Benchmark
99 White Plains Road
Tarrytown, New York 10591-5502
www.marshallcavendish.us

Library of Congress Cataloging-in-Publication Data

Otfinoski, Steven.
Alligators / by Steven Otfinoski.
p. cm. — (Animals animals)
Summary: "Provides comprehensive information on the anatomy, special skills,
habitats, and diet of alligators"—Provided by publisher.
Includes index.
ISBN 978-0-7614-2930-2
1. Alligators—Juvenile literature. I. Title. II. Series.
QL666.C925O84 2008
597.98'4—dc22
2007025448

Photo research by Joan Meisel

Cover photo: N. Reinhard/Peter Arnold, Inc.
The photographs in this book are used by permission and through the courtesy of:
AP Images: 34. *Alamy*: Peter Horree, 22; Tom Salyer, 26. *Animals Animals - Earth Scenes*: Fred Whitehead, 14;
C.C. Lockwood, 28, 29, 40. *Corbis*: Michael & Patricia Fogden, 6; Roger Tidman, 11; Kevin Schafer, 12;
Joe McDonald, 16; W. Perry Conway, 17; Raymond Gehman, 20; Philip Gould, 27; Jeffrey L. Rotman, 37.
drr.net: Heidi & Hans-Jurgen Koch, 10, 33; Shaun Van Steyn/Stock Connection, 21;
Tom Salyer/Stock Connection, 24. *Minden Pictures*: Heidi & Hans-Jurgen Koch, 9.
Peter Arnold Inc.: Kevin Schafer, 1; Dr. Myrna Watanabe, 7; Ed Reschke, 30; John Cancalosi, 36.
Photo Researchers, Inc.: David R. Frazier, 4, 39; Art Wolfe, 32. *SuperStock*: Len Villano, 18.

Editor: Joy Bean
Publisher: Michelle Bisson
Art Director: Anahid Hamparian
Series Designer: Adam Mietlowski

Printed in Malaysia

1 3 5 6 4 2

Contents

1 Survivor of the the Dinosaur Age

Millions of years ago, dinosaurs, or huge *reptiles*, roamed the earth. Though no one knows for sure what happened to them, most of these monstrous animals mysteriously died off. One group of reptiles from the age of dinosaurs survived—the crocodilians.

There are four branches of the crocodilian family: crocodiles, caimans, gharials, and alligators. Crocodiles live in Africa, Asia, and Australia. Caimans, sometimes spelled caymans, live in Central and South America. Gharials, sometimes spelled gavials, live in India and Malaysia, and alligators live in North America and China. There

Alligators are part of the crocodilian family and have been around for millions of years.

Gharials live only in India and Malaysia.

are two *species* of alligators—the American alligator and the Chinese alligator.

The Chinese alligator is smaller than the American alligator. It grows to be no more than 6 feet (1.8 meters) in length and weighs about 100 pounds

6

(45 kilograms). Unlike the American alligator, it has no webbing between its toes. It lives only in the lower Yangtze River valley of China.

The Chinese alligator gets its name from the fact that it can only be found in China.

Species Chart

General Characteristics

◆ The male American alligator grows to an average length of 11 to 12 feet (3.4 to 3.7 m) and weighs 450 to 550 pounds (204 to 249 kg).

◆ The female is rarely more than 9 feet (2.7 m) long and weighs about 160 pounds (73 kg).

◆ The American alligator lives in the waterways, swamps, and marshes of the coastal southeastern United States, mostly in Florida and Louisiana.

Male alligators can weigh up to 550 pounds (249 kg).

A close-up look at the thick, rough skin of an alligator.

When an alligator loses a tooth, a new one will grow in its place.

The alligator looks like a big lizard. The word alligator comes from the Spanish word *el lagarto*, meaning the lizard. This is what the early Spanish explorers called them when they first saw these startling creatures in the lowlands of Florida. The alligator's thick body is covered with armorlike plates. Its long jaws are filled with anywhere from seventy-four to eighty sharp, cone-shaped teeth. Its eyes stick out like bumps above the skull, allowing the gator to see above the water while the rest of its body is submerged. It has four short, powerful legs for walking on land and a thick, long tail that it uses to propel itself through water. The alligator is the only

11

Did You Know . . .
The deinosuchus, the largest prehistoric crocodilian, grew to be about 33 feet (10 m) in length. The largest modern alligator on record was 19 feet, 2 inches (5.8 m) long and was caught in Louisiana.

There is an easy way to tell an alligator and a crocodile apart. When a crocodile's mouth is closed, the upper and lower teeth can be seen.

crocodilian that must live in a subtropical or temperate climate. For this reason, it lives the farthest from the equator of any crocodilian.

People often confuse alligators with crocodiles. While they look very similar, there are some important differences. Alligators have a wider, shorter snout than crocodiles. When alligators shut their jaws, only their upper teeth can be seen. When crocodiles close their jaws, both their upper and lower teeth can be seen. Crocs are mostly a light brown color, while gators are mostly a grayish black. Most alligators live only in freshwater, while most crocodiles live only in salt water. Finally, alligators are less active and less *aggressive* than crocodiles. However, that does not mean they cannot be dangerous.

2 Ferocious Predators

It is a quiet, sunny afternoon on the river. A fat frog is basking in the sun on a lily pad. It keeps a steady eye out for *predators* that may attack it. The river is empty except for a twisted old log that is floating by. The frog relaxes. Suddenly, the log comes to life, snaps open its jaws, and lunges at the frog. The poor frog has no time to hop away and is swallowed whole by a hungry alligator.

The alligator relies on its body *camouflage* to creep up on its prey. It floats underwater or on the surface with just its eyes peeking out. An alligator's vision is sharp, and it can even see in the dark

An alligator sneaks up on prey by swimming with just its eyes above water level.

Alligators have unique eyelids that help keep the eye surface clean.

because the alligator's eyes reflect any existing light and glow red. The alligator can even see its prey with its eyes shut. Special eyelids admit light, allowing the gator to see through them. The alligator actually has two different sets of eyelids. One set moves up and down. The other moves sideways across the eyes. They clean the eye's surface like a car's windshield wipers.

While the alligator eats frogs and other small prey, such as fish, clams, insects, and snails, it eats larger prey, too. This includes large fish, turtles, rats, and even raccoons and deer. When it comes to very large prey, the gator faces a problem. While its jaws and sharp teeth are perfect for catching prey and killing

The diet of an American alligator is varied and includes fish.

An alligator's large jaw helps it eat animals that are bigger than the alligator itself.

it, the gator is incapable of chewing. It can swallow small prey, such as a frog, whole. But how does it eat a deer?

The alligator clamps its jaws on the large animal's leg or another part of its body and drags it underwater, where it soon drowns. Then the alligator rolls its own body until the large animal's body tears away

18

from the leg in the gator's mouth. If it is unable to do this, the alligator will stay near the dead animal until its flesh is rotted and soft enough to tear off. Eating rotten meat does not bother the alligator. If live prey is not available, it will eat the *carrion* left by other predators. In fact, the alligator will eat almost anything, including other alligators. There is no need to get too worried, however. Alligators rarely attack or eat humans.

All this tearing and pulling puts great stress on the alligator's teeth. It is common for an alligator to lose several teeth during a fight with large prey, but the alligator is not worried. Its teeth grow back soon after they are lost. An adult alligator may produce fifty or more new sets of teeth in its lifetime.

Swallowing animals is one thing, but how does an alligator digest the hard shell of a turtle, the scales of a fish, or the feathers of a bird? An alligator's body produces powerful digestive juices that break down these substances in its stomach. The *gizzard*, a part of the stomach, is where the softened food is ground up and digested. The alligator will swallow stones or pieces of wood that then line the gizzard and aid in the grinding process.

Alligators depend on the sun to warm their bodies.

Did You Know . . .

If no stones are available, an alligator will swallow other hard objects to help its gizzard grind food. These objects include shotgun shells, pieces of glass, and even golf balls!

The alligator is a cold-blooded animal. That means most of its body heat comes from external sources. The only way it can warm up is to lie in the sun. The alligator does this early in the day. When the sun gets too hot, the gator moves into the shade or takes a dip in the water. When the sun is lower in the sky and not so strong, the gator will bask in its rays some more.

The alligator lives much of its life in or near the water. The gator thrives in swamps, wetlands, lakes, ponds, and rivers. When water is scarce during hot weather and wetlands turn into dry land, the gator will dig a hole so deep that it is below the waterline. The hole will then fill up with water. Gator holes can often reach a width of 30 feet (9 m) and a depth of 15 feet (4.5 m). If deep enough, the hole will continue to hold water even during a drought.

Alligators live the majority of their lives in or near water.

An alligator hole is the place where the animal spends a majority of its time.

The alligator may spend a year or longer making its hole and then spend much of its life inside it. When inside a gator hole, the gator does not have to go after its prey. Its prey comes to it. Birds and small animals come to the hole to drink or to swim and can be caught and eaten. The gator does not eat every animal that comes to call, however, and the holes are an important part of the *ecosystem*, providing homes for many insects, fish, birds, and small animals. During the wet season, plant seeds that are preserved in the gator holes will help bring new life to the wetlands.

A gator hole is made only for the gator that created it. Gators are solitary animals that live alone—except for a female when she has her young— and they like it that way. Each adult male, called a *bull*, creates its own *territory* in which it lives. It will *bellow* to warn other males to stay away from its territory. If an intruder ignores the warning, the resident bull will hiss at it and chase it away. Serious fights over territory between males are rare. Sometimes a bull will bellow to attract a female in order to mate.

3 Protective Mothers

The months of April and May are the mating season for alligators. Adults do not mate for the first time until they are about eight years old. Bellowing is not the only way a male bull attracts a female to his territory. Special *glands* release *musk*, a powerful, sweet-smelling substance that will also draw the attention of a nearby female.

Before she decides if an alligator is the right mate, the female will give the male a few shoves to see how strong he is. If he appears weak or too young, the female will not mate with him. She wants a strong male who will help her create strong and healthy babies.

To attract a mate, a male alligator rises up, bellows, and vibrates the water's surface.

During courtship, alligators may reach out to each other.

If the male passes the test, courtship begins. The two gators slap water at each other with their heads or rub each other's snouts and necks. Another favorite mating game is for the male to blow bubbles in the water, surrounding the female. Finally, mating occurs in shallow water.

Once the mating period is over, the two gators usually go their separate ways, although sometimes the male remains near the female for months. One month later the female makes a nest for her eggs. She carefully chooses the place to build it. It must be on high ground, safe from flooding. She makes her nest big—18 to 30 inches

(45 to 76 centimeters) deep and up to 7 feet (2 m) wide. It can take her up to two weeks to finish it. The female lines her nest with grass and other plant material, then digs an egg chamber in it. This is where she lays her eggs. Alligator eggs are white, have a leathery shell, and are a little bigger than a hen's eggs. She lays between fifteen and eighty eggs and then covers them with dead plants to keep them warm and safe. Like most reptiles, the female alligator does not sit on her eggs. She lets the sun *incubate* them for her. During the nine weeks of incubation, the mother never strays far from the nest. She guards the eggs from raccoons, snakes, and other predators that would eat them if given a chance.

An alligator nest can hold up to eighty eggs.

Finally, the day of hatching arrives. A baby gets a little help breaking out of its egg from an egg tooth, a short tooth on the end of its snout that helps it break out of its leathery shell. The newborns, called *hatchlings*, are about 8 inches (20 cm) long and have yellow stripes on their backs. These stripes gradually disappear as they grow older. The mother carries her hatchlings in her mouth to the nearest body of water. They dive right in, knowing how to swim at birth.

The mother will stay around to protect her young from predators, including other alligators, for up to a year and a half. If danger threatens, a young gator will chirp to warn the others and alert its mother. She

This baby alligator is just starting to hatch.

Once her babies are born, the mother alligator protects them. Here, the two hatchlings ride on their mother's head.

will scare off the intruder by inflating her body so she appears bigger. If necessary, she will attack and fight. Despite all her efforts, predators will manage to kill and eat nine out of ten young alligators before they reach one year of age.

Hatchlings that do survive double in size during their first year. They will continue to grow about 1 foot (30 cm) each year for about five years. After that, females grow more slowly. Males continue to grow at the same rate for a few more years. In the wild, an alligator may live for up to forty years. In captivity, where they are safe from the dangers of the wild, they may live for fifty years.

Did You Know . . .
Baby alligators stay together for protection for the first year or two in groups called *pods*.

4 King of the Swamp

In 18 million years, the alligator has hardly changed. It has had no need to do so. Its body and features have served it well for all that time. It has not needed to adapt to changing climates and environments as many other animals have had to.

As a predator, the alligator has little competition. Most other large predators hunt on dry land. Other water predators—such as sharks and whales—live and feed in saltwater seas and oceans. One of the few freshwater animals that competes with the alligator for food is the river otter. However, there are too few of those animals to seriously compete for food with the greater number of alligators.

The alligator has hardly changed in the millions of years it has been on Earth.

The alligator's sturdy body has held up well in its struggles with prey and other dangers it has faced. Alligators have been known to survive for years with such serious injuries as missing legs and jaws and broken backs.

Even though the alligator is tough, it does have enemies. One of the few animals the alligator has to fear are poisonous snakes. When preying on such

The river otter competes for food with the alligator in freshwater.

snakes, alligators can be bitten and injected with the snake's deadly *venom*. However, the alligator's skin is so tough that it is difficult for a snake's fangs to penetrate it. Still, there is one predator that almost brought the alligator to the brink of *extinction*. That predator is humankind.

5 Alligators and People

Many people are afraid of alligators. They think alligators will attack them on sight. This is not true. If you leave an alligator alone, it will usually leave you alone. They are afraid of humans and will avoid them. Still, their behavior, as with any wild animal, is unpredictable. People are advised to stay 15 feet (4.5 m) away from an alligator in the wild. Actual attacks on humans are rare, but they have been increasing in frequency as more people move into the alligators' habitat. From 2001 to 2006, ten people in Florida were killed by alligators.

In order to protect both the alligator and the passing cars, police block off a street to let an alligator cross.

Hunters go after alligators for their skin, which can be made into shoes, bags, and belts.

Did You Know . . .

Alligator meat is highly prized by people of the Southeast and is sold in restaurants. The tail is considered the best cut of meat from an alligator.

People have been killing alligators for sport, for their meat, and for their skins for hundreds of years. The tough, smooth belly skin of gators has long been used to make such products as shoes, boots, wallets, purses, handbags, and briefcases. Between 1865 and 1960, people killed about 5 million alligators in Florida and Louisiana alone. The alligators were in danger of becoming extinct.

Finally, in 1972, the U.S. Fish and Wildlife Service declared the alligator an endangered species. Hunting alligators was banned entirely, and so was the selling of alligator-skin products in the United States. Other countries also banned these products.

Over the next decade, the alligator population rebounded. By 1977 there were so many alligators that they were taken off the endangered species list and placed on the threatened list. At the same time, limited hunting of alligators was permitted again

A man at an alligator farm looks after a new hatchling.

in Florida and other states. The sale of alligator-skin products was also allowed. To ensure that the alligator population would not be threatened again, people opened alligator farms in Florida and Louisiana. There, alligators are raised, some to be harvested for commercial products and meat, and others to be viewed by the public in shows and displays.

While the outlook is brighter for the American alligator than for any other crocodilian today, these reptiles still face problems. Alligators are losing their habitat. Swamps and wetlands have been drained to create dry land for development. The land is used as sites for houses and commercial buildings or for farmland. Alligators are being forced to look for new homes. Many of them wander into developed areas, creating a nuisance and sometimes a threat to humans. In southern Florida, alligators have been found living under cars and houses, on golf courses, and even in swimming pools!

When the gator loses its habitat, so do many animals that serve as food for the gator. Hungry, desperate alligators raid people's garbage cans in search of food. When no other food is available, alligators even eat each other.

Many alligators lose their habitats when swamps are drained for new farmland.

Did You Know . . .
The Chinese alligator has not enjoyed the same type of comeback as the American alligator. Today, there are only about 140 Chinese alligators left in the wild. They are the most critically endangered reptiles in the world.

With houses popping up on or near alligator habitats, an alligator on someone's front lawn is becoming a common sight.

Another threat to alligators is pollution. Industrial and agricultural waste and sewage have been dumped into the rivers, streams, and lakes where alligators live. The waste poisons alligators and their environment. Pesticides and herbicides have also polluted waterways used by alligators. The government and private enterprise are working to end pollution and clean up the environment to save the alligator.

Despite these problems, the future looks bright for the American alligator. Today, there are about one million alligators living in Florida alone. With a little luck, this fascinating animal, which has lived on Earth for more than 200 hundred million years, will be here for a few million more.

Glossary

aggressive—Forceful; prone to attack.

bellow—To give a loud cry or roar.

bull—An adult male alligator.

camouflage—An act or technique used by animals to conceal themselves by blending in with their surroundings.

carrion—The rotting meat of dead animals.

ecosystem—A way of life or community formed by the interaction of a group of animals and plants with their environment.

extinction—The state of no longer being in existence.

gizzard—The lower stomach of alligators and other reptiles that grinds food so it can be digested.

glands—Organs of an animal's body that make and give out substances.

hatchlings—Newborn alligators.

incubate—To promote the development and hatching of an animals's eggs by keeping them at a suitable temperature.

musk—A strong-smelling secretion produced by the glands of certain animals.

pods—Small groups of baby alligators or other animals.

predators—Animals that prey on, or eat, other animals to survive.

reptiles—Members of a group of animals that includes lizards, crocodilians, turtles, and snakes.

species—Groups of living things that share the same characteristics and mate only with their own kind.

territory—An area that an animal lives in and defends from other animals of the same kind or species.

venom—A poisonous fluid that some snakes inject into their prey to kill it or to defend themselves.

Find Out More

Books

Feeney, Kathy. *Those Amazing Alligators.* Sarasota, FL: Pineapple Press, 2006.

Halfman, Janet. *Alligator at Saw Grass Road* (Smithsonian Backyard). Norwalk, CT: Soundprints, 2006.

Rockwell, Anne. *Who Lives in an Alligator Hole?* (Let's-Read-and-Find-Out-Science). New York: Collins, 2006.

Snyder, Trish. *Alligator and Crocodile Rescue: Changing the Future of Endangered Wildlife* (Firefly Animal Rescue). Richmond Hill, Ontario, Canada: Firefly Books, 2006.

Trueit, Trudi Strain. *Alligators and Crocodiles* (True Books). Danbury, CT: Children's Press, 2003.

Wexo, John Bonnett. *Alligators and Crocodiles* (Zoobooks). Poway, CA: Wildlife Education, Ltd., 2003.

Web Sites

Alligators: Everglades National Park
http://www.nps.gov/ever/eco/gator.htm

Animal Bytes: American Alligator
http://www.seaworld.org/animal-info/animal-bytes/animalia/eumetazoa/coelomates/deuterostomes/chordata/craniata/reptilia/crocodylia/american-alligator.htm

The Gator Hole
http://home.cfl.rr.com/gatorhole

Gators!
http://www.ecofloridamag.com/archived/alligators.htm

Index

Page numbers for illustrations are in **boldface**.

About the Author

Steven Otfinoski is the author of numerous books about animals. He wrote five books in World Book's award-winning Animals of the World series. He has also written *Koalas*, *Sea Horses*, *Skunks*, and *Hummingbirds* in the Animals Animals series. Steve lives in Connecticut with his wife, a high school teacher and editor.